## PRAISE FOR *TALKING BACK TO THE EXTERMINATOR*

"Ezra Pound asked for a poetry 'austere, direct, free from emotional slither,' poetry 'harder and saner' than the usual fare of his day. I thought of this several times while reading, and being struck hard by, Daniel Bourne's *Talking Back to the Exterminator*. But how is it, I kept wondering, too, that such unrelenting poems wherein even light is smoke, and children are murdered, and 'any second you can be struck dumb,' and memory is an 'exposed metal' that rusts, and monsters haunt us within harrowing experiences of family members, that there can still be...beauty? Or maybe sublimity is the right word, with the sublime's indwelling dimension/stain of darkness? The horror and beauty of, just to name two of many poems, 'Still Life With Susan, the Killbuck Marsh' near the beginning and 'Magnolia Winter' near the end are stunning. This whole substantial collection is unified by Bourne's austere (that realistic and cautioning word again) descriptive power and his refusal to look away, not to evade what has wounded him and wounds us into the poetry of his and our lives."

—William Heyen, National Book Award finalist for *Shoah Train*, author of *Nature: Selected & New Poems 1970-2020*

"In Daniel Bourne's *Talking Back to the Exterminator*, the creatures of the earth are taken on as celebration, rather than menace, where 'bees start to walk/ across the scratched wax of the table...' Bourne is an excellent eco-poet whose poems include—just to name a few—snapping turtles, pheasants, orioles, the extinct Aurochs, groundhog, cows, frogs, carpenter ants, locusts, slugs, skunks, mosquitoes, ticks, and fleas, not to mention 'Great auk. Heath hen. Akialoa./ Passenger pigeon.// Bachman's warbler. Carolina parakeet./Labrador duck." Bourne's poetry is also rooted in place and memory, in such riveting poems as 'Autobiography with Line-Breaks,' while others remember toy guns and spit baths. He is a poet who writes out of the personal but whose astute gaze is outward towards the world, towards our perilous future. *Talking Back to the Exterminator* is an extraordinary collection."

—Denise Duhamel, author of *Scald* (2017), and *Blowout* (2013), finalist for a National Books Critics Circle Award

"In *Talking Back to the Exterminator*, Daniel Bourne finds himself in the liminal spaces, between humanity and nature, city and country, present and past, the living and the dead. In poems by turn sharply observant, starkly unsparing, and bracingly humble, Bourne draws these realms closer. This scion of farmers, this longtime sojourner of language, furrows these pages with the plowshare of poetry: 'On the page, the farm can flourish./On the page, my dad still lives.'"

—Philip Metres, author of *ShrapnelMaps*, NEA and Guggenheim Fellow

"Daniel Bourne situates us among a world of near and far neighbours, and of ancestors moving from Ohio to Illinois for over a century before his 'returning' to Ohio and making it his home. In this book of intense localism fused with journeys away and journeys (even if he ponders 'Against Travel' and the depths of staying home) into the interior of land, family, and the stories around these, we receive an intense dose of the rural, the natural world, and what threatens it externally and internally. But if the local world is at the core of Bourne's sensibility, then its peripheries are diverse, from the world and works of Borges and tea ceremonies to developed considerations of signs and works elsewhere. There's a powerful series of childhood evocations, and renderings of historical moments, often immersed in a tension between locals and the natural world. But there is a generous infusion of swamp deer and cardinals, of animals, plants, and birds amidst the vulnerability of a world on the edge. Violence, extinction, and loss threaten the familiar, and the familiar is imbued with an anxiety about its presence. A poem can move from celebratory observation to deep scrutiny in a moment. The familiar so often contains the unexpected.

—John Kinsella, author of *Peripheral Light: New and Selected Poems* (Norton), editor of the *Penguin Anthology of Australian Poetry*, founding editor of the literary journal *Salt*, and former international editor of the *Kenyon Review*

"Daniel Bourne's *Talking Back to the Exterminator* sifts through layers of both smallness and occasional grandeur—insects, birds, isolated people dotted about a dusty landscape toiling until they die, the stories of Borges, the teachings of Jesus. Who are we at our center and how are we alike? the poems inquire through trails of velvet ants and lost dogs and bad weather that gets inside the house. 'I don't want to speak too fancy here but this bird is an artist,' we are told about juncos after a thunderstorm, and this is the reliable magic of these poems: the comfort and insight they pass gently to the reader without making a big deal about it. I will return to this book often to be reminded how to imagine the world from the inside out."

—Lisa Lewis, editor *Cimarron Review*, NEA Fellow, and author of *Silent Treatment* (Viking/Penguin), National Poetry Series Award-Winner

# TALKING BACK TO THE EXTERMINATOR

Daniel Bourne

Regal House Publishing

Published by
Regal House Publishing, LLC
Raleigh, NC 27605
All rights reserved

ISBN -13 (paperback): 9781646034819
ISBN -13 (epub): 9781646034826
Library of Congress Control Number: 2023942955

Cover images and design by © C. B. Royal

Regal House Publishing, LLC
https://regalhousepublishing.com

The following is a work of fiction created by the author. All names, individuals, characters, places, items, brands, events, etc. were either the product of the author or were used fictitiously. Any name, place, event, person, brand, or item, current or past, is entirely coincidental.

For Margaret, for her ghosts as well as mine

# FOREWORD

*by Abigail Warren*

Daniel Bourne's well-crafted poems, with his close watchful eye, take the reader through the natural world, while quietly interjecting the human eye on what he sees. With straightforward diction, his words, poems go straight to the heart and head. His graceful intimacy invites us into the small daily pleasures and complications of everyday life. Daniel pays attention to not only the natural world but the looking, the observer. This is a bold, passionate collection, startlingly honest, and always with the sweet, gentle touch of the human heart.

Moreover, Daniel Bourne indicts himself in this complex world, as any strong poet must, but does so with an understanding he, too, is part of something larger, as in "Close Neighbors." It reminds me of *Jude the Obscure* and Jude's same observation:

> But maybe
>
> it is a time for a shaking of the head,
> to give sheepish thanks
>
> that the child is not ours.
>
> But he is. He lives on this street
> like we do. He pesters the bird nests
>
> in the tree in our yard.
> We should call his father to complain
>
> but the yelling coming from their windows
> is our yelling too.

He does this again in the poem "Talking Back to the Exterminator," as he questions what to do about a swarm of yellow jackets in the eaves of his home:

> And what would this mean? that the swarm
> would one day fall out ...
>
>  but still—
>
> And then you shake your head. It would be
> a visitation, you say. This home
>
> is large enough to contain others.
> So why should we complain if the bees start to walk
>
> across the scratched wax of the table,
> through the sticky rooms of our bodies?

As Daniel Bourne's poems take us to various landscapes in his rural homeland, his family, one can't help but think of Seamus Heaney's poem about his father, a fine potato farmer, but Heaney will learn to dig with his pen. So, too, Daniel will learn to work the land in a multitude of ways:

> But I won't sell my land just yet.
>
> This is why I still open my mouth.
> On the page, there is no stutter.
> On the page, the farm can flourish.
> On the page, my dad still lives.
>
> On the page I plant things.

One of my favorite poems, "Wild Onion, Easter Sunday," holds Bourne's keen observations of the natural world. It is almost prayer-like, and perhaps no accident the title holds

Easter Sunday with each word calling out to him, calling out to us. The poem holds an intimacy between Daniel and the Lenten world—springtime and the lengthening of days. We, too, smell the wild onions, and the rich earth he walks upon. The internal rhyming, the lovely sounds between the words "wood" and "anemone," and "marsh" and marigold." And the soft vowels of "trampled wild onion." There is so much to love in this collection; Daniel is a poet of the elements, finding significance in the slightest gestures; a necessary reminder of who we are, why we're here, and where we are going in each bountiful, precious day.

> …Spring beauty,

> wood anemone, marsh marigold,
> dwarf ginseng, squirrel corn.

> Only the sharp scent
> of trampled wild onion

> brings us back to the weight
> of our bodies, to the mud

> smelling up our hands…

Abigail Warren lives in Northampton, Massachusetts, and teaches at Cambridge College. Her work has appeared in numerous literary journals and magazines and her essays have been published in *SALON* and *Huffington Post*. Her book, *Inexact Grace* (Regal House Publishing, 2021), was a finalist for the Terry J. Cox Award, and *Air-Breathing Life* (2017) was nominated for the Massachusetts Book Award.

# CONTENTS

*Talking Back to the Exterminator*

Close Neighbors . . . . . . . . . . . . . . . . . . . . . . . . . . . . . . . . . . . 11

Talking Back to the Exterminator . . . . . . . . . . . . . . . . . . . . . 13

After Supper . . . . . . . . . . . . . . . . . . . . . . . . . . . . . . . . . . . . . . 14

A Long Way Across the Fields . . . . . . . . . . . . . . . . . . . . . . . . 15

In the Place of Reading the Classics . . . . . . . . . . . . . . . . . . . 17

The Good Daughter . . . . . . . . . . . . . . . . . . . . . . . . . . . . . . . . 20

The Interior . . . . . . . . . . . . . . . . . . . . . . . . . . . . . . . . . . . . . . . 22

Near the House . . . . . . . . . . . . . . . . . . . . . . . . . . . . . . . . . . . . 23

Wild Onion, Easter Sunday . . . . . . . . . . . . . . . . . . . . . . . . . . 25

Still Life with Susan, the Killbuck Marsh . . . . . . . . . . . . . . . 26

Secrest Arboretum . . . . . . . . . . . . . . . . . . . . . . . . . . . . . . . . . 27

Instinct . . . . . . . . . . . . . . . . . . . . . . . . . . . . . . . . . . . . . . . . . . . 29

The Safety of the Trees . . . . . . . . . . . . . . . . . . . . . . . . . . . . . . 30

Arch Deluxe . . . . . . . . . . . . . . . . . . . . . . . . . . . . . . . . . . . . . . 31

Before the Next Damn Thing Comes . . . . . . . . . . . . . . . . . . 32

Definition . . . . . . . . . . . . . . . . . . . . . . . . . . . . . . . . . . . . . . . . 33

Outings . . . . . . . . . . . . . . . . . . . . . . . . . . . . . . . . . . . . . . . . . . 35

On the Border of New York and Vermont . . . . . . . . . . . . . . 36

Margaret Madly Weeding . . . . . . . . . . . . . . . . . . . . . . . . . . . . 38

Jewel of Bohemia . . . . . . . . . . . . . . . . . . . . . . . . . . . . . . . . . . 40

The Life-List . . . . . . . . . . . . . . . . . . . . . . . . . . . . . . . . . . . . . . 42

The Last Bestiary . . . . . . . . . . . . . . . . . . . . . . . . . . . . . . . . . . . 43

Against Travel . . . . . . . . . . . . . . . . . . . . . . . . . . . . . . . . . . . . . 44

Snow Moon . . . . . . . . . . . . . . . . . . . . . . . . . . . . . . . . . . . . . . . 46

Ambush Predator . . . . . . . . . . . . . . . . . . . . . . . . . . . . . 47

Flood Stage . . . . . . . . . . . . . . . . . . . . . . . . . . . . . . . . . 49

In Charcoal, in March . . . . . . . . . . . . . . . . . . . . . . . . . . 50

The World Writ Large, Writ Small . . . . . . . . . . . . . . . . 51

A Tropic Benediction . . . . . . . . . . . . . . . . . . . . . . . . . . 52

The First of October, We . . . . . . . . . . . . . . . . . . . . . . . . 54

### Interlude of 12 × 12s (Part 1)

Red Sky at Night . . . . . . . . . . . . . . . . . . . . . . . . . . . . . . 59

Abandoning the Nest . . . . . . . . . . . . . . . . . . . . . . . . . . . 60

Cuneiforms . . . . . . . . . . . . . . . . . . . . . . . . . . . . . . . . . . 61

At a Rest Stop Near Lake Erie . . . . . . . . . . . . . . . . . . . . 62

The Winter Too Soon . . . . . . . . . . . . . . . . . . . . . . . . . . 63

North of Niagara…I Think of Dead Actors . . . . . . . . . . . 64

Tea Ceremony . . . . . . . . . . . . . . . . . . . . . . . . . . . . . . . . 65

### But You, Borges, Unabashed

Plato's Groundhog . . . . . . . . . . . . . . . . . . . . . . . . . . . . . 69

Borges, Looking at His Shelves of Books . . . . . . . . . . . . . 70

Last Gestures . . . . . . . . . . . . . . . . . . . . . . . . . . . . . . . . 72

Patron of the Arts . . . . . . . . . . . . . . . . . . . . . . . . . . . . . 74

Beatitude . . . . . . . . . . . . . . . . . . . . . . . . . . . . . . . . . . . 76

One's Tongue . . . . . . . . . . . . . . . . . . . . . . . . . . . . . . . . 77

A Small Prayer . . . . . . . . . . . . . . . . . . . . . . . . . . . . . . . 78

Absinthe . . . . . . . . . . . . . . . . . . . . . . . . . . . . . . . . . . . . 79

Girl with Bird . . . . . . . . . . . . . . . . . . . . . . . . . . . . . . . . 80

To the Extinct Aurochs of Europe . . . . . . . . . . . . . . . . . 81

Contact . . . . . . . . . . . . . . . . . . . . . . . . . . . . . . . . . . . . 82

The Gleaner's Song . . . . . . . . . . . . . . . . . . . . . . . . . . . . . 83

The State Trooper Submits His Report . . . . . . . . . . . . . . . . 84

Fallen Timbers . . . . . . . . . . . . . . . . . . . . . . . . . . . . . . . . . 85

Student Bride, Indiana University, ca. 1929 . . . . . . . . . . . . . 86

A Man Stacking Stones . . . . . . . . . . . . . . . . . . . . . . . . . . . 88

The Gifts . . . . . . . . . . . . . . . . . . . . . . . . . . . . . . . . . . . . 91

The Obligations . . . . . . . . . . . . . . . . . . . . . . . . . . . . . . . 92

Car Trouble, Henry Mountains . . . . . . . . . . . . . . . . . . . . . 93

The Evacuee, Chiricahua Mountains, 2011 . . . . . . . . . . . . . 94

The Dwellings . . . . . . . . . . . . . . . . . . . . . . . . . . . . . . . . . 95

Counting the Coral Beans . . . . . . . . . . . . . . . . . . . . . . . . . 96

Royal Gorge, Arkansas River, 1959 . . . . . . . . . . . . . . . . . . . 98

## Interlude of *12 x 12s (Part 2)*

To the Old Country, Illinois . . . . . . . . . . . . . . . . . . . . . . . 101

Mangoes . . . . . . . . . . . . . . . . . . . . . . . . . . . . . . . . . . . . . 102

Between Fields . . . . . . . . . . . . . . . . . . . . . . . . . . . . . . . . . 103

Dead Weight . . . . . . . . . . . . . . . . . . . . . . . . . . . . . . . . . . 104

Cave Painting on the Inside of My Skull . . . . . . . . . . . . . . . 105

In the Last Days, Cardinals . . . . . . . . . . . . . . . . . . . . . . . . 106

## *The Rinsing*

Autobiography with Line-Breaks . . . . . . . . . . . . . . . . . . . . . 109

The Alien . . . . . . . . . . . . . . . . . . . . . . . . . . . . . . . . . . . . 111

The War Home . . . . . . . . . . . . . . . . . . . . . . . . . . . . . . . . 112

The Rinsing . . . . . . . . . . . . . . . . . . . . . . . . . . . . . . . . . . . 113

We Were Going to the Devil . . . . . . . . . . . . . . . . . . . . . . . 116

On Having a Manger in Our Family Barn (Near Wynoose,
    Illinois) . . . . . . . . . . . . . . . . . . . . . . . . . . . . . . . . . . . . 118

Stigmata, At Seventeen . . . . . . . . . . . . . . . . . . . . . . . . . . 119

Spit Baths. . . . . . . . . . . . . . . . . . . . . . . . . . . . . . . . . . . . . 120

All Souls Day, Illinois . . . . . . . . . . . . . . . . . . . . . . . . . . . 121

Legacy . . . . . . . . . . . . . . . . . . . . . . . . . . . . . . . . . . . . . . . 122

Yes, to the Mole, Emerging in Night . . . . . . . . . . . . . . . . 123

Lizzie Bourne Above the Treeline, 1855 . . . . . . . . . . . . . . 124

Spoon River, Personal Mythology, 1988 . . . . . . . . . . . . . . 126

In the Bottomland. . . . . . . . . . . . . . . . . . . . . . . . . . . . . . . 128

After Eden. . . . . . . . . . . . . . . . . . . . . . . . . . . . . . . . . . . . . 129

Dense Ground. . . . . . . . . . . . . . . . . . . . . . . . . . . . . . . . . . 130

Magnolia Winter . . . . . . . . . . . . . . . . . . . . . . . . . . . . . . . 131

Achilles in the Fence Row. . . . . . . . . . . . . . . . . . . . . . . . . 135

Ant Farm, Ohio. . . . . . . . . . . . . . . . . . . . . . . . . . . . . . . . . 137


Acknowledgments. . . . . . . . . . . . . . . . . . . . . . . . . . . . . . . 141

# TALKING BACK TO THE EXTERMINATOR

# CLOSE NEIGHBORS

These are the adjustments: hot day in October,
we string thin white wires on our porch

to hold the climbing roses

that have climbed all summer, waving their twisted arms
at bare ankle and fragile wrist, each thorn

unsure if its greatest loyalty is to the sap
inside its own body,

or to the summoning of blood from us. In any case,

it is our turn to tame, to cut with abandon,
because they climb where we don't want them.

Meanwhile, the neighbor's small kid, liquored up
with the chemicals he was born with,

roars up our street and onto our porch, an oak branch

in his hand. *This is a gun,* he says,
*and this is how I will kill you,*

and then he yells and runs off.

It's a time perhaps for laughter, for the joy
of once more encountering violence

only through the imagination. But maybe

it is a time for a shaking of the head,
to give sheepish thanks

that the child is not ours.

But he is. He lives on this street
like we do. He pesters the bird nests

in the tree in our yard.
We should call his father to complain

but the yelling coming from their windows
is our yelling too.

# Talking Back to the Exterminator

We were warned.  The queen
could bury herself in the yard and the swarm

of yellowjackets would return to our eaves
next year, their forays

into the unseen parts of our soffit, a small hole
in the wall bitten through, and soon there would be

more avenues for their kind
than rivers in North America.

And what would this mean? that the swarm
would one day fall out

through the roof of our kitchen, a stormy god, like all gods,
not meaning harm, not necessarily

meaning anything, but still—

And then you shake your head. It would be
a visitation, you say. This home

is large enough to contain others.
So why should we complain if the bees start to walk

across the scratched wax of the table,
through the sticky rooms of our bodies?

The doors so small
we will never pass through them.

# After Supper

Two figures on the garden stones, the slow
sweep of their footsteps, the one talking
is out of breath, winding down

but has to keep going
the last few steps to home, his words'
slow climb to my apartment window

like the last sigh of the day's heat.  I can tell
he wants to stop talking, but can't.
And as the other person turns away,

out-of-patience or a desire
to put away her shovel, I start
to clear the table, to erase

the awkward conversation
I have had with my own life, this confused
sacrifice of root vegetables and meat

I keep stirring on my plate.  Meanwhile, the birds
continue to sing, or at least I start
to notice they are singing, that my mouth

is motionless at last.  Every day
I must learn again
how to find my real food.

# A Long Way Across the Fields

Through binoculars we watch the horse being buried,
backhoe dig its teeth deep into the sandy earth
as the John Deere that pulls the Great Belgian carcass
circles the hole till the tumble occurs just right.

And that is that. The other horses already
led to the pasture on the next hill. Who knows
if the owner wished to spare them the viewing? This owner
a far neighbor we have never called by name. So why

do we watch, eyes fixed on the last
flash of yellow flesh, lightning bugs gladdening the field
in between? Do we want to see our own death
cast in such slow, deliberate motions, the end hitting

us so firmly and squarely those standing nearby
will also be astounded? Last year our neighbor
hit his head on his porchpost. But his funeral
did not delay our vacation, although my wife

held his head in her arms till his family arrived,
Margaret repeating his first and last name
*Emmitt, Emmitt Austin,* the way you might like to have
your own name said, a delicate grace note

in the middle of the last song sung on earth, a quick
swinging of the heart, impatient stamping
of hoof in soft dirt, such a soothing sound,
yet everything heard so badly,

so far off, you wished it could be repeated
over and over again
until we could all agree
on the small thing that we have heard.

# In the Place of Reading the Classics

I only wanted to change the firepit
the old bricks and cinder block construction

decayed from the heat of too many times
I drank Scotch and doggedly burned our pines

which climbed too high for their own good
and snapped off in the west wind

that rose up from the low dip of land in the horse pasture.
Our green neighbors to the south had it worse, burning

the slumped trunks of downed oak leaves, inhaling
the vapors of poison ivy vines so hardy

an itchy-palmed Tarzan would learn, eventually,
not to swing from them

even to save Jane from the jaws of factory outlets.
Day after day the smoke would rise up. Day after day

I would think to go over and meet them.
But this didn't happen until later,

until their hard work was done,
and now I hope they forgive me, scratching

at the welts on their calves and ankles.
But we all have our own hidden cargo.

The granite for our fire pit
carried in the bellies of glaciers

to New England, then hauled in a semi
to a big wooden pen in Ohio, a giant pasture

of other stones, the true nature
of decorative rock. Then, by Jeep bed,

it was onward to our garden
where I tugged them out and rolled them to nestle

in a clump, cheek by jowl by cheek.
I had just given birth to a litter.

I had just robbed the stone aerie
of the Phoenix. She

would soon find me. But she
would burst into flame, too. Every fire pit

a new beginning, the ongoing
death of the world. And each time

I burn out here, I think
of my own lungs, tiny caves

collapsing around the edges,
thin balloons

swelling up with smoke, the heat increasing
until the pressure ruptures the walls

and the sea swamps in on the land. Meanwhile,
I listen for my mother-in-law's cough

as she dreams of the dust inside our house
that never quite manages to settle, or my wife,

waving from the porch, forever on her own,
weaving her many frayed woes from yet

another hard week of work, the words of her boss
like a new version of the end, until

miraculous and sheepish as always
I emerge from the fire and the smoke,

open my mouth and try to speak.

# The Good Daughter

## I.

The rain collects. The cellar
filling first

through the broken
mason jars on the floor

until a foot
slaps on one step,

and the next,
groping up to the light switch—

## II.

The good daughter hollers
for her mother to run. But

there is so much to save. Each table
seats three or four chairs. Each chair

with porcelain setting before it.
Each piece of china

covered with spoons and sharp knives.
Each knife pointed

at her own heart. Each spoon loaded,
overflowing.

III.

The good daughter cannot save
even two of each kind. She

cannot save her mother
dragging the sofa

from the buckled wall,
or while she rolls up the carpet so massive

that no one can lift it. Only so much
can fit in one hand

and with the other
climb the antenna to the roof, pausing

on each rusted spindle
at her mother's stream of words:

*Keep going. Go on. Without me.*
*Come help me with this. Where are you?*

The river's belly heaving
so close beneath hers. The helicopter cameras

mere inches from her head.

# THE INTERIOR

You wake me with a bad sore throat.
The furnace has made the air too dry.
Your voice cracks, the wood settling in the house

cracks, the sound of metal scratching
on metal goes up through the heating ducts. I
should go to the kitchen, bring you oranges,

boil water to steam up the room. But I don't.
I just listen.  The house breathing in,
breathing out, waiting

for me to make the next move.

# Near the House

Try to explain this. A pheasant by the road
sees our car, but does not start up. Instead,

the iridescent throat heaves, the swept-back wings cock
themselves as if the pheasant

is just asking for battle,
as if our red Jeep is just a big galoot

heading straight into his territory; blessed, his own.
Later, the long slow throat of the evening

gathering around us, we see another male pheasant
pecking his way along a cornrow. Is he

looking for the last kernel, the first
sign of a female? All these nerves so het up

and we, driving along so slowly,
swerve a little to the left

and a car behind us tries to pass
like buckshot let loose from behind a fencerow

follows up the long rainbow feathers of the tail
full bore, just missing the small blinking head,

just missing the left side of our car
as the driver opens up his door, now

slowing down, ahead in the road, wanting
us to stop and get out

because he thinks we almost killed him,
because he wants his great due. Yes,

to participate in this ritual of greeting
of the middle finger, the cock

of the walk. So much ground
we want to call our own.

## Wild Onion, Easter Sunday

We skirt the buttonbush swamp
rejoicing in the early spring

lack of leaves, the sunlight
able to reach

all the delicate wildflowers
with their even more delicate names,

just too good
for the usual earth, spring beauty,

wood anemone, marsh marigold,
dwarf ginseng, squirrel corn.

Only the sharp scent
of trampled wild onion

brings us back to the weight
of our bodies, to the mud

smelling up our hands.
Our field guide says

a fen flushes,
and I say

even more blessed is the bog
stewing in its juices

forever and ever amen.

# STILL LIFE WITH SUSAN, THE KILLBUCK MARSH

What we feed on
feeds on us.

The dead turkey sprawling the ditch,
the mosquitoes

lapping at our shoulders
as the swamp spreads out

in the tangled feathers of darkness.
Our craw

can process anything
and our bones

down the maw of this swampy road
will come out somewhere

intact and glorious. Not
that we have died. But that we

have lived at all.

# SECREST ARBORETUM

Siberian larch, Tamarack, Norway
spruce, Boxwood, Bourne. Yes,
I too am a transplant, the journey

to Ohio, the tongue
of the root system tangling
as it learns a new word for soil.

The vowels between the skinny leaves
and pliant needles. The consonants
like slight grooves in the bark.

Who knows the stories these trees
could have had? The Siberian larch,
its fate sunk down in Ohio

in 1915, just escaping the Russian Revolution,
the silent parade of men beneath its branches
with guns pointed at the backs

of other men. The Norway spruce
forming the great backbone of a house
destroyed by saturation bombing. The boxwood's

deeply concentrated grain
hard to chop down, though its branches
will gladly sacrifice themselves

to the topiarist's delight.
The tamarack brooding on the edge
of a cranberry bog. —And Bourne?

One ancestor came in 1838 to Ohio
to build a canal, but left soon after
to farm in Illinois.  And his great-

great-grandson comes in 1988
to settle here, ten years later,
on the first green grass of late March

to look up in the branches
of another type of family,
its arms opened in welcome,

in blessing.

# INSTINCT

A small car, and a big snapping turtle
laying eggs in front of its bumper

as we turn a corner
in the Killbuck Swamp. This boy

looking through the windshield
of his rusting Plymouth

doesn't move an inch. He's here
on this planet

to protect this clutch of eggs,
or at least

to wait decently
for the turtle to finish

before he kills her
for grilling or for soup.

But the turtle
is oblivious:

her hard beak
curved like the earth.

Big paws scraping
through the gravel

the local township
deposits each spring

to try and stop the mud.

# The Safety of the Trees

We've all seen that same bird
make for the treeline

the gunsights trained

as if a world can be created and destroyed
that quickly.

But the bird

doesn't know
if this next breath, this next

pump of wings

will be its last act or not, its legs
finding purchase, the blood

migrating

the well known routes of its body.
Or if it will slam down

in the hard November field, giving

much joy to the dirt clods around it,
which never

ask questions, which gladly

take advantage of any drink
offered

to slake their constant thirst.

## Arch Deluxe

Underneath the billboard's proclamation
of the newest version of meat

the carcass of a deer
mashes down the oil-browned leaves by the roadside

its neck
curved back over its small, athletic shoulders

as if mesmerized
by the late autumnal migration

the mixed herds of cars and semis
pushing on to their November feeding grounds

but many
will have to drop before the night is over

to pull into the pockmarked parking lots
and amble up to the counter

eyes blinded
by the sudden light.

# Before the Next Damn Thing Comes

Plastic beer cups in weeds
as if souls could be caught on camera

desperate to rise
above the ditches of the Lakefront.

The smell of tailgate picnics
abandoned, in regret

not for the home team losing
as all home teams must lose,

but for this Sunday
and no other, the life worth living

displayed on a platter.
For a moment

everyone knows their place.

# Definition

It was not a Japanese painting.
We were in bed, Mary Chapin Carpenter

and her soft flannel shirt of a voice.
The moon did not exist

except when we looked at it
which was often.

It climbed, full-bellied, its light
all the more blinding

when it ended, the tear
that creates the fabric's true character. No wonder we

have always said Swiss cheese. The mares
of the moon with their deep dark ninny,

the sea horse of our neck
not knowing which way to go.

Should I kiss you, here on this always awkward planet,
the surface

covered with the slight depressions
of sleeping cats. Or

should my mouth, round and open as its subject,
point upward

to the one desired thing
every surface on this earth

moves towards in dark and light. I
could say all sorts of words here.

# OUTINGS

The surface of the pond so brown the boat's
two oars look like they rot some more each time
we dip one in, we don't come here to fish
but to feel the July sweat dig deep inside

our own small mouths, hook on and lift us up
from our own dank and troubled skin. Meanwhile, our son,
fingers smeared slightly with earthworms,
sits there poised, scanning the water

for a fish to come and galvanize his life. But we
have no illusions. To breathe with lung or gill,
to hook or get the hook sunk in us. It's all the same.
To watch the snake swim into shore, its wet

black rope of skin a question mark. What next:
to look at you and see your hand is webbed?

## On the Border of New York and Vermont

Just a few inches away in the car
my wife dances the hula
to a Rascal Flatts song,
no grass skirt
but her hands wave

the sweep of green hills
as I shift into low,
the front of our car

plowing the upland waves.
We are between civilizations,
from one island to another,
small town shamans, sheepish

flatland animals of the Midwest
digging hard our canoes
crossing over the reef.

Voyage of strange
portent. It goes on. These hills
like climbing bar chords. A good
strong hand to clamp the strings.

Before us archipelagos of clam chowder,
lagoons of stone walls,
white clapboard houses unfurling the starch
in their sails. All in a swoop

and dip of Margaret's hands
as the Rascal Flatts guy
drives his voice off the road

but swerves back just in time.

# Margaret Madly Weeding

Some of them she even knows by name
and some of them not, her gloved hand briskly yanking
the necks off of multiple lives. Margaret

is madly weeding. She grips the tops, the tresses
of the ecumenically christened
but invasive Bishop's Weed,

whose rhizomes build a city where only
it can worship. The grid of death.
The end game in the church of summer.

Margaret is Conan the Barbarian.  She is also Kawaii Cute. Yes,
I am looking at the naked part of her foot, the dull brown
    leather strap
against her white ankle. I think of her in bed and her feet

spread across the rumpled sheets.
Earlier, she showed me favor, her display
of wearing her babushkas, power cloth

swaddling her head like Rosie the Riveter or Rachel Carson
or the bandana crosswise like a roaming pirate—
the creator and the destroyer
the revelation of all her beautiful names:

*Margaret Milkweed, Sock Monkey, Queen Mab, Baba Yagi, Goddess*
    *Mamuszka, Naga Małgorzata.*

These are her names. Repeat them if you will.

You will love her. I will love her. The weeds will love her.
The weeds whose fate she decides
by squeezing their green stems.

# JEWEL OF BOHEMIA

No one thinks of Noah at night. Forty times
he floated into darkness. There

before the happy ending of doves and rainbows
was the lantern made of garnet

he held in his hand
as he ministered to the animals, telling them

memory was even more powerful
than promise, trusting

the creatures' old worlds
of grass and nest and burrow

would light the growing flood
of darkness. Yes, as you read this

yours is the stone
that has always guided travelers; the heart's

own light
that you carry. O Jewel of Bohemia, red

pomegranate, your own crystal seeds
refracting the past and future, every facet

like the surface of a planet, the wax and wane of waters,
little girl walking through the weeds, the world of pale Ohio

that years later, you make into your garden,
red gem of tomato and strawberry, or the balm

of catnip
to administer to the last days of our black diabetic cat,

the flood of blood and urine, the covenant
that we should have

with all animals, to make them feel,
like we do, that we will live forever, the kind delusion

that God will never
do this same thing again. That is why you whispered

those memories to your father, the old
words of Bowling Green and Jerry City

so that he could once again wade through the gathering
of ivy, his own Ohio flood

of childhood, Black Swamp,
wet desert, land of sogginess and need. Near death

he opened his eyes and saw not just the ceiling
but through your bright swaying lantern of words

he heard the snap of locusts in the beech trees, Joyce and Betty
calling him in to supper,

fried pork and pickled beets. The pigeon near the barn
bearing branches for its nest. Land at last nearby, the boat

nudging up on shore, though all around,
of course,

was darkness.

*(For Margaret, born in January)*

# THE LIFE-LIST

Beyond the next fenceline
the extinct may be watching.

*Great auk. Heath hen. Akialoa.*
*Passenger pigeon.*

*Bachman's warbler. Carolina parakeet.*
*Labrador duck.*

They notice our small markings:
bronze rivet on denim, the small

cracks in the leather jacket,
the plush velour

of an untied housecoat. Each sighting
one more for their life-list—

though we are so plentiful
our flocks cover the sun, nests

clogging each lakeshore, the Great Plains diminished
to a rhizome of roads.

The flashy wing-bars
on a shoe, the colored beaks of our SUVs. Yes—

*Great auk— Heath hen—Akialoa—*
checking off your name and your name.

And mine.

# The Last Bestiary

When all animals have died
even the ones in books

grow frightened, their eyes
like wormholes. Their spines

not so much broken, but the hide
abraded and peeling. The gutters

filled with debris,
plucked feathers, old yellow tape.

No one was there
to hear their last song.

And in between the last pages
were two old brown leaves

speaking in a language
only other brown leaves would know.

# AGAINST TRAVEL

". . .we must tend to our own garden."
———Voltaire, *Candide*

With the dog's burrs so goes the world.  Batavia,
New York, the lawn of the Best Western
seamless with the Thruway, the cars
mere inches from our noses as we take

our dog Nashville for a walk. He is in need
as all dogs are—not just to use the bathroom
but to feel that this
is his life too. His planet. Tongue

falling out, he looks back, then races
straight for the shallow ditch,
a row of purple loosestrife, spiked
helmet of invasion. No insect or deer

can stomach it. But it looks so beautiful
people from Albany or Buffalo
dig it up and bring it home. Perfect
for the garden. Soon

it will be the only thing alive. And now our dog,
so happy, travels through its blooms, the seeds
commandeering his gray Schnauzer coat
for the ride to New Hampshire, to our sister's

unsuspecting home.  O Nashville
I would like to blame you. You
stupid fool. Your dubious honor
of being our unwitting friend. There

are too many of us. Too
many of you. O Nashville,
how soon for us to learn
to stay in one place and be content?

# SNOW MOON

Late February, El Niño's warm breath
has melted the snow
on the sleeping neck of Ohio. Skunks

waddle from their burrows, sniff
at the neighborhood dogs. The stink
of small fires burning in the weed beds

climbs up towards the dad
carrying his drowsing son to the porch,
the boy's shadow bouncing, bouncing.

Beyond the porch is mud, the moon's
shadow finding only mud. The small
stripes of snow in the midst

of so much black. The warmth inside the house,
the warmth inside the flannel that the boy
dons before he climbs into bed, the black

warmth building towards the coming
waves of summer, the evil-queen
prick of mosquitoes and all the ticks and fleas,

Zika and West Nile. The bed bugs in his dreams
sucking towards their own hunger.
Sometimes we need the cold

to kill what's killing us.

# Ambush Predator

From the cemetery the brown pit bull lopes out
as if to bite our tires—or leap into our laps

ecstatic to be saved from its abandonment, but we
are already scooting down the road, the dog

shrinking smaller in the mirror—a panting, upturned stone.

We drive on the edge of the Killbuck swamp, the notorious
    swamp,
abandoned refrigerators mixed with sphagnum moss,

tundra swans and raccoon hunts, the muskrats
always eying their holes in the bank. We wonder
if this dog is local, a canine psychopath,

broken off his chain and roaming
like a lion to recover his pride, crazed

because of the years anchored to a concrete slab

and now wanting to chomp some havoc
for the degradations done to him. Yet
not all pit bulls are monsters, and maybe this lop-eared galoot

is just another body dumped beside the garlic mustard,
victim of yet another summary judgement on this planet

delivered by a hard hand. *There you go doggie. Go eat some
    ducks or die.*
But the language is not so harsh

when the land itself speaks. The hope still surging forth
from the ballooning throats of spring peepers

to coax out their own type of love
from all this muck. Who knows what will kill us

or let us alone, the eagle's nest next to the herons
does not mean the rookery is doomed,
while who can stop the small fry from darting

inside the crevice of a hungry lunker's mouth? Once I saw
a movie filmed in the forest tangle of Ecuador

some tiny hatchling open-mouthed in a nest,
its neck stretching up like a rubber band
towards the hovering bird it thought must be its mama.

A hungry baby who could not wait to be fed.
And then the larger bird gobbled it up. Who knows when

we will eat or be eaten. If the next guest I let inside my door
will be a hell-hound

or my last friend on earth. No wonder
that when the jaw opens

it is so easy to hear the groaning hinge of the world.

# FLOOD STAGE

Early March, little white ice floes
bob like flocks of seagulls
in the Killbuck Creek floodwaters. But no,

those are real seagulls out there, a little
lost on their way to Lake Erie, dazed
in the sudden glare. All night I heard ice

turn to drips and then rivers, our basement
flooding, sopping white typing paper
and styrofoam popcorn, the alluvial

slime at the bottom of the stairs.
Meanwhile, seeping through the drywall
the ululations of Ocelot our cat

with the need to wreak destruction
gushing from his throat.  He
has seen through the window

the white bibs
on all the lovely sparrows
and wants so bad

to kill them, his claws
unfurling
like the first crocuses to appear.

# In Charcoal, in March

To the left of the road, a small stand of maple, buckets
like ghosts in the twilight, small drip
of this past year

boiled down to sweetness local priests
used to call the soul, a dark velvet wafer
to put on the tongue and then forget.

Not too much farther
and we will reach Apple Creek, the slow Amish buggies
on their way home from Troyer's pie store, the horses morose

in the late afternoon glare. So much
blackness and blindness. No bag of oats
in the barn will soothe them. This

is what we were born
to talk about, the ring we build around us
this year, neither wide

nor narrow, the slow murmur
of one season to another, craning our necks north
to the herons' nests clumped on Barnard Road, black village

nodding in the tops of even darker trees. All this
condensing down to the sweetness
in word after word, testament growing

like a fog that closes in, blessing
each surface it can touch, each opened cup of earth
into which it will collect unseen until we drink.

# THE WORLD WRIT LARGE, WRIT SMALL

Late October thunderstorm, over the barn to the west
the sky managing a dark gray with whitening belly

the hard slap of rain on the sides of the propane grill
already rusting like the exposed metal that we call memory

and then I see the little storms hopping along the edge of the
    garden arbor
the gray and white juncos just arriving from the north

riding the winds in from the boundary waters little feathered
    canoes
I don't want to speak too fancy here but this bird is an artist

they don't need to sing because their bodies move like music
all winter composing their little black grace-notes

scoring the tops of the deep and dirty snows

# A Tropic Benediction

Each carpenter ant a small lightning strike,
by the end only the bark held the tree together.

In the middle of the night, the middle
of Ohio, on midsummer's night eve when the trees

are supposed to be worshipped, their insides
released on hilltops, the breath of earth a slow burning,

the state trooper dispatched to the scene said
we must remove it from the highway *A-SAP*—as if

she too were writing a poem, *A-SAP*,
learning the local tongue, drawing each word from the roots,

trunk and fork, limb and burl, the count of each
ring of words to see how harsh the weather was that year.

But she just wanted to get the road cleared,
so out came the chainsaws and we entered into the hard

thighs of branches, the limp hair of the
already dying leaves, wading through the downed lines

we could only hope were dead. Power
out in the neighborhood, we felt our stiff muscles

take up the flow, chopping and hauling, stacking
and sweating, touching each surface of the tree as if

it were an instrument we were playing,
a saint's bones to finger, a tropic benediction

on the first summer solstice of the last
century we will ever know—farewell to the oak

who blessed us with its last four years of life
and when it let go it wanted humans to take heed,

to roust the dreamers from their beds and stop the night-
hauling semis cold. But it spared each tree around it, the sap

in each aspiring trunk like high voltage wires continuing
to sing above our heads. A sop of current. And flowing slow.

# THE FIRST OF OCTOBER, WE

Suddenly we can say *last month*,
that small flip of calendar between us,
September 11 now out of mind
at least in the way we might want it,
somewhere beyond, not quite reaching
here to the swamps and Amish of Ohio
the way Kafka's imperial messenger,
by the end of the story, never
quite arrives and we have to dream
the emperor's last words, the first instructions
in this new world no one thought would happen.

The icon of the month: Dalmation
to Schnauzer, alpine lake in Colorado
to an autumn hayfield in Vermont,
April's swimsuit model and the endangered
species for May. A bomb made
from a jetliner hits the World Trade Center
in New York City. A jet plane flings
a bomb on the Taliban in Kandahar. These
are the transformations of the world,
one thing leading to another, one god
picking up the phone and phoning
the second god, saying hey you
keep the racket down. Meanwhile,

we also want to put down distance,
get away from collapsing shard and myth.
We want to speak metaphorically
and not then have someone die. We want

the person next to us to be
our neighbor. We want to turn to them and say
remember. We want the version of the fable
where we have still survived.

# INTERLUDE OF 12 x 12s

## (PART 1)

# RED SKY AT NIGHT

Red sun, red barn, the squeezebox of cows at milking,
field in between white with the lazy winter paint
of snow, and right then the dog takes off for the woods,
his leash flapping around his neck and suddenly

we imagine his death, the car bumper slamming
or the slower, more pitiful version: his whine
as his leash gets snagged on a log and his hunger
eats him like the mice inside a burlap sack. Then

you sigh. How long will this go on? Our sense of loss
ready to bellow as the cows who need the pull.
And is it relief or routine washing over
as our dog lopes up with his black flag of a tongue?

# ABANDONING THE NEST

The wasps dab at the window, black wings transparent
in the sun. Through the miracle of glass, I watch
as their abdomens aim towards my hand, stingers

so close I can detect their throb and ache. I too
would try everything, fling myself towards the paw
that swipes both food and beloved young. But I mean

no harm. I'm just here, my chitinous fingers poised
as if to dance with the heated swarm. Soon enough
the first hard frost will come, my own son covering

up his ears in bed, while all viable wasp eggs,
sweet little chiclets, will peep out their sad, sad song:
*Abandonment. Abandonment. Abandonment.*

# CUNEIFORMS

Cove in bay, and frog in snake, the chewed stick my son
throws in the fire. Wet flame of this day, flames eating
other flames, small rivers meeting the big rivers,
the orange part of the oriole meeting the black,
roots like smoke finding passage through the rock, the sleeve
inside out on the scratched back of the rocking chair,
which my mother picks up and looks around for me.
(There is not much time to remember this.) Her child
fallen down a well or just sleeping in his bed.
And this jacket she picks up to her nose and smells.
One room and then another, fading ghost of my
own son's flashlight, as he reads the walls of my brain.

# At a Rest Stop Near Lake Erie

The birds suspended in the trees, up and down, not
like musical notes, since they themselves are playing,

but up and down nonetheless, the kohl-eyed kinglet
a nervous actor in the cottonwood's first green bursts

along the Crane Creek boardwalk, the vast migrations
of birders and their multi-colored license plates

settled in for a morning of dog-eared field guides
with cracked spines, spotting scopes trained on the brown
    brocade

back of a chuck-will's widow strayed so far off course
it will never make it back. But sometimes no one

can get to there from here. (*As if our own hard skin
could bloom in feathers. Our callused throats burst to song.*)

# THE WINTER TOO SOON

The water to the top of the fenceposts, and then
it froze. I imagined the swamp deer, hooves sliding
over the roads of barbed wire buried beneath, fields
still great with corn. I imagined Dickie Walker
putting down his gun to climb over the frigid
lip of ice, and the bullet that blew off his nose,
the way he cradled it in his frozen mitten
as he stumbled back to his truck, raw meat preserved
by the raw cold. Yes, they were able to put it
back on, a red lightning slash on each side, God's sign
that, any second, you can be struck dumb, the trap
slathered with the bait, your tongue frozen to its teeth.

# NORTH OF NIAGARA, BRUCE PENINSULA, I THINK OF DEAD ACTORS

*Zoo-Zee Zoo-Zee Zoo-Zee,* feathered Cary Grant, black-
throated green warbler not quite getting the pitch, pine-
jumping along the escarpment, C-130
troop plane hard on the throttle, on practice patrol
over Whipperwill Bay; or, really searching, eyes
peeled on some stranded boat in Georgian Bay, the next
shipment of Lake Huron ghosts to the ancient falls
buried at the end of the last Ice Age, brooding
to this day of their own demise, white dolomite
and plush guzzle as the engine labors so hard
just to keep itself aloft, the call of songbirds
drowned like back at our old farmhouse in Ohio

these same gray planes ungainly as school buses banked
just above our roof, all the roar and squeal after
September 11, National guardsmen from Kent,
Macedonia or Mansfield, hurtled into
the cobbled web of this war. *So how can there be
un-self-conscious metaphors here?* The cliff face mere
inches from our feet, our necks craning out to get
a better look at these rock climbers to the east,
their spiderly ambition so frail against stone,
our mind's dour web filmed in black and white, last night's
    dream
of my son's smile as he leaped off the balcony.
Like Fred Astaire—though I know I tell it badly.

# TEA CEREMONY

It is only tea on the table, but I watch
the curved handle of the cup, the white porcelain
of your palms like the inside of an oyster shell,
the word *china* like a pearl's slow build up until
the mouth is opened and jewel exposed. *The word is*

*and is not the flesh.* It is not that we drink tea
but that we dream life into this vapor. *To bite
the tongue from the corpse*, yet spit it out like a boy
siphons illicit fuel. Even to touch their books
Tibetan monks had to wear gloves: the paper thick

as a hornet's nest made from their own saliva,
then coated with strychnine to stem the hungry worms.

# But You, Borges, Unabashed

# PLATO'S GROUNDHOG

I'm the groundhog, but I'm late.
Long past February, still in my room.
Before my burrow the spiked ice drips.

Everyone else plays in the sun.
But I'm not budging. For months
I ate for two. For this big pelt of fur

and its shadow. Now,
I take it easy. I know
I can always flip the latch, go out

and proclaim the next six weeks
winter or spring, my blind divination
of the world others see so clearly.

## BORGES, LOOKING AT HIS SHELVES OF BOOKS

Even the dying man in the story
could look. His final vision
on this earth: the spines

of the volumes he had written
tormenting: more and more pages
of clutter,

more surfaces
of the brain, more trees
to fall in the forest so that in the city

the people could read.
So the scholar passed away—
his book burned, forgotten,

or ignored. But you,
Borges, unabashed as a young girl in Indiana
learning to speak Latin,

run your fingers over each of your shelves;
your book, someone else's book. It doesn't matter.
They are all worth reading, even in braille,

and who cares if the list of named things
will grow even longer, that each line of poetry
will fall from the cliff of the page; you

the celebrator of knives as well as of libraries, cut,
and cut deeply—and are glad you have cut—
here on the bus tour

of the Afterlife, eyesight restored, elbowing
Milton or Homer, smiling at all
the strange things by the road. Even Helen Keller

can't keep from laughing. She who from the start
had the most sense of all. She who felt the water
fall from the pump

—and said *water*. She who had found
the perfect word to say.

# LAST GESTURES

*If the world would end tomorrow, I would*
*still plant my apple tree.*—Martin Luther

It's not that you knew
each other. Sylvia, you never sat
for the *Tischreden*, an acolyte
recording Martin's every word, greasy spätzle

dribbling down his chin as he complained
of the devil farting on top of a drainpipe
just outside his casement window so loud it was hard
to hear God.

*Aber Sylvia, auch du*—years later
the books and bobby pins of your own life, preserved
in the sour aspic
of reading rooms, the red crayon blouses

of the paper dolls you made
pinned back around the throat. Even the insides
of the dust jackets of the books you owned in college
offer up the runes

of your now long-dead desire, the Viking Library's
list of published classics, little white boxes nailed
with the black smack of your fountain pen:
*Which of these books would you like to read?*

And now all this talk—not so much about survival,
but about our last gestures on this earth, when
there are apple trees to plant, root vegetables
to prepare for our children, the need to peel

and boil. Sylvia, did you stick a fork in to see
if the carrots were soft
before you turned off the burner
and opened up that blessed oven door?

# PATRON OF THE ARTS

The small dog in the corner of the painting
is not sure about the hand stretched down.
It may be Jesus or a dog catcher

but the dog doesn't know. And you also
have yet to make your decision,
to stand and bite or slink away.
The loose board in the fence is the only
friend that you can trust. Meanwhile,
your eyes forsake the edifying foreground.
The saints with their ravaged faces,
their writhing robes and wrists,
slope up past snaking alleyways
to blank adobe, to bare vineyards and small streams
to a man and donkey on a far hill, wishing
they walked in the direction of their only meal.

All the world that should be attending
the center panel now turn away
to their own tiny miniatures of history—
spear and ploughshare, marriage
and manger scene, museum gift-stop and buffet—
as out in the far-flung plains
your own kids deny their childhoods

too many streets away, tiny figures glimpsed
so far off you cannot tell
which way the body bends
although it always seems to droop to earth.
And then in the middle of the gala,
the angel hair pasta tangled in your teeth,

the parquet floor beneath you
unlearns its tongue and groove,

and below a soup of monsters
gape up with dislocating jaws,
their tongues like tiny pitchforks
murmuring in the mess
of steam and scudding cloud:
*Thank you for your kind donation.*
*We are ready now to eat.*

# BEATITUDE

Blessed are the effigies, even the most scrawny,
for they shall inherit the earth—the stuffed
rooster, claw missing, the eye a blue marble
aimed toward the backyard, where the flock
eats to this day, the sun going down
the gullet, getting stuck
in the maw. When the father came home
all the children scattered, their small bellies
fragile, their T-shirts extravagantly painted
as the Easter eggs at church. But that of course

is when the real scratching begins, the turning over
of each stone by the porch, not even pausing
to inspect the bugs first, but just to eat of the bounty.

*Later, while sleeping, was the rooster done in.*

But is this the fable we all want to hear,
the orthodoxy tossed into the cradle
just to quiet the baby? Whose hand was it
that grabbed the neck, twisting the comb
until the eyes saw all,
saw nothing? And what settled
there in the dust, the small mites
crawling on feathers and the mites
crawling on other mites? Each speck
must find at last a place to land, each feather
hearken back to the plucked and disbelieving body. Yes,
the rooster was raised up, dead and crucified, preened
for veneration even as its white parts and dark parts all fried.

# ONE'S TONGUE

Who will eat the small god?
Its jar

open in the corner. Your child
mouths

the one word it knows. A second

word quivers nearby, but that
is still too far away, the hunger of the last animal

to arrive at the manger, the grain
giving out in the most fertile fields, the curtains swaying

even though the wind lies exhausted in the ditch:

the mud cracked into small countries invading each other
the small particles of meat that resurrect to form religion.

# A Small Prayer

This small flock of birds
in an even smaller tree.

This small dish,
poison to those who taste it.

This small descent
when the knees start to buckle.

This small wrapper
of the sour candy of the heart.

This small medicine
we swallow once a life only.

This small difference
between predator and prey.

This small dog.
This cat the small enemy of the dog.

This small piece of paper.
And you the small god,

listening to the prayer.

# ABSINTHE

Inside the wormwood of Europe
the compressed grain

sharp blossom of mold
in the moored boats

the edges of the harbor
where the deer drown—

such leeches
even the priests cry out

the father's cough
his own child eats like

an obedient carp

# Girl with Bird

*(Nationalmuseet, Copenhagen, August 2008)*

Was this girl cast into the bog
on the Isle of Sejerø

obedient—
or did she forget to bite her tongue

in the presence of her elders

one day at the well
when she waited with her heavy jar,

twisting little rings in her hair.
Either way

the mud closed in,
the bones of a small bird

placed inside
her permanently outraged mouth.

Her body

the only language of her village
that did not go extinct.

# To the Extinct Aurochs of Europe

I think of the baroque writing
of their horns

twisting on the river's smooth mud.

The pack found them
in the shallow water of the bog.

Afterwards, man
and his most beloved beast

enjoyed the dark caves of their marrow.
Companions

whose language
we still try to speak:

the teeth of the dogs

carving their first stories
in the waiting page of bone.

# CONTACT

For days the plates waited, little ghosts in the dark,
their tightly packed bodies.

Then the fingers came, and one by one each
was taken away, but never

was the curved edge of the survivors
imagined to be a smile.  Once

a mouse died in a teacup
but no one knew

except for the teacup.
Out in the parlor

there was much talk about someday
putting down new contact paper, something

with red ladybugs, their antennae
tuned sharp as piano wire.

But the people had their own problems.
Soon they were waiting in silence—

little ghosts in the dark—
as the strangers came and banged upon their door.

## The Gleaner's Song

I love it when the light
slides sideways, mouthing the tops of the downed
bottomland stalks, flutes
splintered as if music could be tongued and slathered

like a dog trying to get at the cake of marrow. Sideways, too,
the straps of the backpack
blow in the playground's gale, the sway
of swings just one more sign the children will be abandoned

soon after the party in which they
will be sung to around the cluttered table
as if they are the precious one. Last night in the frost,
the bluebirds joining in a knot, though their blood still
    succumbed

to the crystal lullaby of ice. All this to confirm
that while you stoop to pick the scattered seed, to live
is to keep singing, your lips still trying to coax
the song from out of your mortal jug.

# The State Trooper Submits His Report

This is the ramp, overgrown with pigweed and jimson,
the black gas can, abandoned. The next

turn off doesn't come until eighteen miles ahead.
So this is where

it had to happen, the way
a grain elevator explodes, or the oil-soaked rag ignites

up in the horsebarn hayloft, the moment
something inside a stopped man detonates

and seeking salvation his fingers
fondle the black trigger beneath his seat.

(Last night I expected to hear
the high whine of the cornpicker's auger

that sliced off my father's hand.
We found him with his bandanna

unfolded on the ground.)
But the last thing I will talk of

is how I spent three hours towards morning
searching the ditches

for anything I could find. I found odd shoes
and punctured beer cans.

And lots and lots of weeds. I found water
and bent down to drink.

# FALLEN TIMBERS

And then I was lifted. Of course I saw
nothing, the top of the house
I had only seen in dreams—gasping
as my eyes gazed on all the shingles—
already vanished. The baby I held
was found a mile away,
torn from my arms.

In my legs the splinters
of a hundred trees. After a while,
the doctors sighed and turned away.
Years later, I can still feel the wood
shift in my skin, the sharp jab
and sometimes blood, a ditch
collecting the Black Swamp's rusty water.

At the site of Fallen Timbers, college kids
still find arrowheads and knives
lifting up to the surface. The past
wakes up inside the land. We
are all locusts, emerging,
walking up the trees, our voices
brooding tornados, remembering our own lives.

## Student Bride, Indiana University, ca. 1929

Like anemic raccoon coats, slicked and oily,
the boys' graduation gowns

make them look so listless and puny, black hems
daubing about in the Spring mire.

Two weeks later
we walk through our own muddy yard on Dunn Street

to the wraparound porch, take
off our shoes and unlock the door. We

are home. Each morning,
when Al walks up the street to the bank

I watch him grow smaller, his suit
a precious black dot, the end

of a cheerful old song. I pucker my lips just
to remember the tune. But sometimes

the house around me grows, each room
like a mirror, poised for me to jump through it. Sometimes

I sprout up through the gray tile of our roof.
I look down

at our own small row of yew trees,
each bird nest not quite

so round and safe
as I would like to imagine. Sometimes

when I take up a throw rug
I can only see bare floor.

# A Man Stacking Stones

*(Inspired by a sign at the Cape Coker Community Center, the
Bruce Peninsula, Ontario, mentioning that the stacked stones on
the beach were part of a local self-help therapy program.)*

### I

Here in mist, even
Georgian Bay does not exist, waters

do not exist,
the leaves of trees, the thick trunks

and their own heavy language.

Unfortunately
I have said too much as well.

My hands
speaking a language as I hit her

that even frightened me.

### II

So now I build. This stone
for its flatness.

It will provide the base

for the world to balance—
one elephant leg, testing

the shell of a turtle.

This stone for its color, the
dark bruise of shale. (*Yes,*

*even the hardest rock*
was once just softened clay.)


### III

Each stone,

with its own sins
washed up on the same shore. Soon

my knees will be surrounded.
My back and heart enclosed. The rock

slow to anger, difficult to dislodge.

Soon
the view around me

will only be of stone,
the pockmarked

surface of my skin,

middle-aged dolomite, its pores
enlarging

in the slow fingerings of rain.

## IV

In the middle of Georgian Bay
the water still falls and falls

over the ancient Niagara

before the last glaciers melted
and the pressures shifted elsewhere—

Yes, I too long to be swamped
by a new sea, buried and forgotten.

There I will abide.

Each stone I have chosen. Each
heavy word. —It was

through silence after all

that my own burdens
came to rest on her.

# THE GIFTS

The closet where the black sweaters hang. Where the game of backgammon is played with the thin wafers left over from communion. Of course they break and the crumbs travel everywhere, refugees so small that even the mice turn carnivorous, squeaking with pleasure even though they haven't yet begun to eat.

And how tight will that wire wrap the barbs inside itself? All objects when abandoned develop a talent for self-loathing. If you can't say something nice, don't say anything at all. How else could the elbows wear so thin? How else could the bird fly into your mouth?

## The Obligations

The garden on the side of the house with its yellow patches, the peas not quite right because of the rain and the slugs. Everything that manages to grow gets eaten by the groundhogs or if it lives long enough a stupid deer takes a bite and leaves the rest to spite us. I told my husband and he told our child, but what more is there to say? You either have the dirt inside you or you don't. We coiled and uncoiled the hose for days and still the water refused to bend its neck to our will.

They said put horse manure on the asparagus and we did it. We tried okra but it turned woody and then in the nearby fencerow ghosts started turning up. Our family dogs and the small coils of stories my husband and I could not agree to say. It was like they were hissing. This is what I think about when I plant more things and destroy others. You could call me a god if I were already dead, if I were present in your dreams. But instead I have a trowel. I dig in the rows all day. If you see me from the street, I will wave as if there is nothing wrong, no matter if my fingers are bleeding. Some subjects are better left untouched.

# CAR TROUBLE, HENRY MOUNTAINS

Sand, sego lily, Tarantula Mesa,
And the red light on the dashboard

Throbbing like a flash flood, fifty miles
From the nearest road

That acts like a road, with culverts
And junction signs

For the boat trailers to Lake Powell.
Out here, there is only buffalo shit

From the only free-range herd outside of Yellowstone.
And cactus with water so hard-earned

It wants you to feel pain
Just for the fact you desire it.

Out here,
only your eyes travel fast.

And even they stop dead
After running into stone.

# The Evacuee, Chiricahua Mountains, 2011

All night he dreamed the fire
was on the ridge above him.

The acorn woodpeckers'
eyes wide with alarm.

The white parts of their wings
glowing red from the heat. Each fear

like the round base of a desert spoon
scooping up flame and then tumbling

to ignite the entire grove of oaks
growing to the edge of his water tank.

That is why in his eyes first light
seemed just another type of dense smoke.

In this place, even the resurrection plant
was never coming back.

# The Dwellings

We go down to the place of the high weeds, brown animals
and small sounds that make us think of ourselves and our
   shortcomings.
An old well with its smother of moss, the stones breaking in the
   mouth of the earth.

The rat snake basks on the cracked leather of the car.
Wasp nests in the window like abandoned adobe, the dry season
when the rind of the gourd refuses even

to open up to the boy's knife. I lived there once
but I don't know what happened to the people
who made their objects lie in such a hopeless tangle, the flood

through the canyon pushing one body to another, their small
waists draped in the white arms
of the desert aspen. The red bearded penstemon

cropping up like dragon seeds. It was so hot
but the horned lizard could only
raise one leg up at a time.

# Counting the Coral Beans, Horseshoe Canyon, Chiricahua Mountains

*"The Erythrina seem fine, and are robust as they head into winter. I am praying that we will not have another three-day freeze, and that our field season next year will be like I had hoped, with lots of flowering and a "normal" pattern of growth."*

—Lyn Loveless, Dec. 17, 2011

Scramble up, scramble down, always the worries, the slow chew
of the prickly pear, sudden
strike of a rattlesnake. But usually
it is something

more mundane, the slight twist of an ankle
and a mouthful of dirt, the research assistant
who puts the coral bean in the wrong plastic bag. But even that

is not so much of a disaster, not like the hard freeze burning
the roots of the miraculous plant *Erythrina flabelliformis*
on the northernmost tip of its range. Everything
becomes delicate eventually, dwindles down

to survival strategies, roots living beneath rock, friendships
    forged
over centuries. The ants that protect
from the hunger of mites, and the *Erythrina's* crimson flame
providing them with nectar. But this year after ice

came fire, its quick tongue
grazing the slopes
like armageddon's sheep, nipping off everything green. The
    benches
strewn with black balls of desert spoon
like the heads severed by revolution. Scarred yucca. Black bear
disrupted from their haunts. Smoke
bothering even the trogons in the draw.

Scramble up, scramble down,
through the black ash, counting the coral beans that survived.
There is still always a story to tell, the narrative of biomass
and bean, the battle between ant and moth
you monitor by flashlight. Maybe no blossoms this year,

but life will go on "until it won't go on no more." No wonder
your own roots run so deep, though invisible
beneath your floppy hat
as your hands sweep your flock of students
up and down the steep ravines,
nibbling as they go.

# Royal Gorge, Arkansas River, 1959

Another door slams, another Kodak camera
stuck right up my nose.

I would tell you about my life
but I won't.

But this one white kid
my age, car

license plates from Illinois,
is too scared to walk near me

to get his picture taken
"with the little Indian,"

as his sour-puss sister names me
waving her hand, her hair

yellow as cornmeal.
The feathers

in my hair
are work clothes.

Stories
are what create the skin.

# INTERLUDE OF 12 X 12S

## (PART 2)

# TO THE OLD COUNTRY, ILLINOIS

Devoured? It won't be the locusts who will eat you,
but their song. Row after row, the sparse names of corn
and beans, beans and corn, on either side of the road
as out the window of your car the black fenceposts
start up a strobic motion of their own: movie
made up of the blacktop from Noble to Wynoose.
Uncle and maple, sycamore and aunt. The bridge
over the Little Wabash and the cracked reptile
skin along its banks. Despite even the old words,
it must happen: *You will forget to remember
yet another thing.* Leaf on tree and hole on leaf,
everything cracked and burning, cell by cell by cell.

# MANGOES

Who was to say what was exotic? We called green
peppers *mangoes*, small knife cutting them into cups
then scooping out their sexual innards, white seeds
and tasteless pulp. The green shell a slickened chalice
we would fill with cold water from the dark mother
of our cistern. And sip. Even later, in the
blessed age of cheap Chablis, as I poured my wine
onto Jolene's belly in southern Illinois
I still had the sense of being in the garden,
my Adam's apple bobbing and ready to fall.
It was in that moment, the first unctions of sex,
that my tongue went back to the old language again.

## Between Fields

The infrequent clarities of fencerow. Sometimes
when you think you see light, it's only the silver
bark of the sycamore, pale ghost of the old stream,
bison leg bone and Mound-Builder axe-head. The salt
lick of your own history, and how many times you
return to it, one eye cautious, your tongue lapping.
Ten cents a row, corn knife in hand, from stalk to stalk
you went that one year, slicing the volunteers, green
shoots from old grain scattered in the harvest. And then
you would reach the shade of the fencerow, the small gaps
through which you could spy the next field, the turn of earth
that led to this place where you became crop—or weed.

# DEAD WEIGHT

Think of the dead weight of air, the low slant of sun
that slices through the window, your father out on
his rounds, and you at the kitchen table, writing
your poem. Each step he takes up in the loft might be
his last, and you are writing your poem. Your stomach
sick with the yellow glare, the flies crawling the screen
as the green hay builds up its anger, the seething
that turns into fire, a cave hollowed out not by
water but smolder. It is this way that your world
will burn its own nest. Your father takes one more step
and breaks through the surface. And you would carry him
out if you could. *O stupid son. Draw back your chair.*

# CAVE PAINTING ON THE INSIDE OF MY SKULL

Four men roll the deer over the hood of the truck
and up onto the roof. Almost dark, the orange vests
hover beside the road, like swamp gas, the tender
laying on of hands as one man adjusts the neck
and the slack, exposed belly jiggles to a stop.
This much I know, but then I drive on, the dead deer
still alive for a little while, grazing the edge
of the bottomland fields, wary as it nibbles
at late November's abandoned corn. Soon, the shot
will ring out—and quickly die again. And even
in town, I'll still see the deer, the red neon signs
flashing how blood was our first paint, our first language.

# In the Last Days, Cardinals

The last days should be short, merciful, the wine good.
My parents will come back each morning. Their hands warm
in that tiny kitchen with the wood stove, the one
that scarred my arm. Always there is eating. No one
has to talk. In those days my mother will even
allow our dog inside the house, all snakes outside
to live. Fear and temptation will pass from the earth.
All images will be blessed. The lion lying
down with the soft stubble of the lamb. But I still
worry about the birds, their plans to build their nests.
To gather a twig means no time to find the worm.
Their ode to windows as they attack their own face.

# THE RINSING

# Autobiography with Line-Breaks

## I

I press this paper down
Imagining my father scribbling
With his finger on his knee
Counting acreage and drought,
The math that could not feed us
On that farm he had to sell.

Carter Bourne wrote with his left hand.
He stuttered, words beating like the wings
Of a captured sparrow.
The runt of his litter,

He was not just the youngest son.
He could not hold the twisting horns of his farm.
He could not wrestle the growing weeds of cancer.

## II

Youngest son of a youngest son,
No wonder I tried to be a poet,
Another awkward farmer.
There is pigweed and mares-tail everywhere

But I won't sell my land just yet.

This is why I still open my mouth.
On the page, there is no stutter.
On the page, the farm can flourish.
On the page, my dad still lives.

On the page I plant things.
Straight rows I hope
Will intersect with distance.

# THE ALIEN

I woke up in bed with an alien. Granted, I was just a little boy, and the lump in the blanket may have been the family cat or dog. But, at the time, my mother didn't allow pets in the house.

So I woke up in the middle of the night and there was this alien, this little ridge in the bedsheets. I didn't dare disturb it. I didn't say, "Hey, you there, little alien. What are you doing in my bed?" I was too frightened. I thought that if I would just keep quiet and pretend I didn't see it, the alien would think I was sleeping and leave me alone—and so when I woke up in the morning the little, menacing thing would be gone, having flown back to where it came from, while I would be safe and after breakfast I could go outside and play with the dog as if nothing had ever happened.

This happened over twenty years before Spielberg's E.T. rode a bicycle through the sky with his little white spaghetti fingers. Back then, the Soviet premier Nikita Kruschev was the biggest thing around. Since he was so evil, his big white head on television bobbing up and down like a potato in a boiling pot, since he took off his shoe at the United Nations and banged it on the podium and said *We shall bury you. We shall bury you*, I thought that if the Russians invaded all we would have to do was act as evil as they were, just wrinkle our noses and say words like damn and shit and hell. The Russian invaders would pop out of their tanks and go—*Oh, you're evil too. Our mistake!* And since we were already evil, they would go back to Russia, to their ice and lard and vodka, and we could go back to sleeping safely in our beds and playing with our dogs.

# THE WAR HOME

It was during Vietnam
and I was in my backyard

playing baseball with myself.
I was carrying a gun

as I searched for the whiffle ball
I had slugged near our corn crib.

In the first rows of soybeans
two Viet Cong popped into view—two—

and pointed their rifles at me.
My own weapon jammed

and as I turned to run to the house
I felt two slugs—two—

hit in separate places on my back.
One hard punch. Then two. Afterwards,

 I woke up in Illinois
and lived for decades with these wounds

while boys in rice paddies
dreamed of waking up as well.

# The Rinsing

I don't remember the suds so much but
the scalding rinse water boiled on the stove

poured down on my hair
in that cold Illinois kitchen

my sister's elbows on both sides of me
working the lather

not in but out.
I felt

my sister's body at my back.
Off in the living room

the Vietnam War
was going badly. On the back porch

was what a Charles Dickens teacher
at Olney Community College

would call a chamber pot. I had
a standard ops.

Bare feet could handle
the living room carpet.  Socks for the

cracked tundra
of linoleum in the kitchen.

Shoes to use the pot
on the mud-infested back porch.

Any further, and you had to buckle up
your boots. You had

to empty the pot the next morning. No matter
what was in it. In fact

you were grateful. The rinse,
the cleansing, so close

to the godliness of families
we visited on TV. Or

the more lucky sides of our relatives
with their shag carpet toilet seat.

Sometimes
I'd wait so long I'd carry

Around small clumps inside my pants. Sometimes
I'd turn around

and bite my sister on the arm.
Earlier

than I can remember
they tell me

I'd drop a toy
So that she would pick it up. I'd leap

on sister's
St. Francis of Assisi back.

I'd hang on with my teeth,
This is the way we

lived back then.
This story

is not made up. This
is Danny speaking. I

will not let go.

# We Were Going to the Devil

We were going to the devil,
and I was worried. His office

was nice enough. A door stood open
to the bathroom. Beside the toilet

hung a towel. My dad said
I have to stay on this couch

and then he was led out of sight.
On the wall hung a picture

of a hideous clown.
The red paint smeared

around his mouth like the blood
of the innocent devoured.

*Is this the devil?* I said. *Is he
devouring my father right now?*

When my dad finally re-appeared
we walked out into the sunlight.

*Only one cavity*, he said
and it was then I learned

how language tricks us in the world:
that *devil*

and *dentist*
are not quite the same thing

though the one still leads me
to the think of the other.

# On Having a Manger in Our Family Barn (Near Wynoose, Illinois)

I apologize for the rural imagery
of the bible. The cow who falls into a ditch

on Sunday, the ladder between earth and heaven.
And who needs to know about separating goats

from sheep, the hate of wheat for chaff? Let old wars stay
in the old world. How the Elect will survive

no matter what, the runts of the litter
chewed up by the mother. And while we're discussing

god as memory and as blood, don't forget the story
of the prophet Elisha approaching an isolated town

and the boys cried *"bald head bald head"* before our god
sent a she-bear from the mountains to devour them.

I was a child when I read this. I pulled my own hair.

## STIGMATA, AT SEVENTEEN

I don't have many ghosts. At least very few
care yet to own me. Sailing around

my head in a soft glow,
the after-life neon of a Dairy Queen, small

tremors of the earth, faint omens
of everlasting sex. I am seventeen

and my first girl friend has yet to dump me
while the light of the dashboard that I would like to describe
    as blue

has me fixed in its mother/father gaze and I
am already practicing

what I will say when I get home, inebriated as usual,
to my dead father

and to my mother who will one day be a ghost
about Jane Herschau and her mouth upon my neck,

my first one true love ever, though
she didn't have the decency

to leave a deeper mark.

## Spit Baths

Can we talk now about spit baths?
The mealy touch of the handkerchief
after my mother or Aunt Linda tongued
its corner, the warm saliva washing off

some visible dirt caked at the edge
of my lips. Even then I knew
of the unseen, the sins no ablution
could wash away. But my mother's

spit on my cheek was not in vain. My eyes
closed as she rubbed it in, first known lotion,
first thought of the two-way river of sex,
smell of the interior of bodies, the dried crust,

flood and draught, outward wince and hidden maw of pleasure.

# All Souls Day, Illinois

The next room I sleep in will look out on a yard
where I dance with the ghost of my first childhood dog,
emery tongue and velvet paw, june bugs buzzing
in the bronzed light, the sweet salve of their beneficence
in a world of wasp and the velvet ant
I once followed through the tall grass at the edge of the garage,
my finger measuring the small gap between my skin
and the agony of venom. Meanwhile, beyond the garden,
the sad ghost of my father
takes my mother's hand and sails off over the snarled branches
of the crab apple tree, the locust chorus not so much
     complaining
as incessant that they too will never be forgotten, the slow
emergence of their bodies, green gristle drying on the bark,
and I so young that the fire
was about to erupt from my own skin.  No wonder,
the late summer trees were so noisy, no wonder
out among the tall brooding hoods of corn,
the parallel rows just kept going, beyond fencerows and rivers
until they met together in the tangled infinity of loss.

## LEGACY

In the midst of holy land, a dead sea, childhood
coated in rock salt, each spoke of each wheel, each word, coated,
that enters the shallow floodplain, the roads and crops,
the depression of earth and fault, the physics of sheer and
    thrust,
of blight and pest and rift, coated, the language of your mother
    and father
walking the gravel road, the garden and their death

the way when a tree falls the fence row opens up. Soon,
only your backward gaze will remain. Relic
like shadow. Like Lot's wife
the cast of your long kindness and the sparse herds of goats

that will live long after you. Gospel and psalm
in the long blade of grass and the nibble of the knife.

# Yes, to the Mole, Emerging in Night

Towards the moon we all
move if we can manage it,

our tiny dirt
covered shoulders.

The beauty of earth
as it shrugs off

each direction of the wind.
The small stirrings of our parents

in their last hours.
The sweep of hands

on blankets.
Their fretful, blind

devotion.

# Lizzie Bourne Above the Treeline, 1855

## I

This rock is as good as any
to mourn her, the first stone of the burial mound,

the pillow underneath her head, small shelter
to stop the wind, the free fall

of the temperature of blood.
My ancestor

who will always be a girl,
dead on Mount Washington,

layers of wool and petticoats
soaked with snow and trapped sweat

weighing her body down as she climbed
to the most extreme weather

in her bare corner of the world, her
quiet clamor in my mind

as I hike up the Ammonoosuc Ravine
on a bright August day almost a century

and a half later, my own sweat
tasting like a penny in my mouth, a sign

the weather is so gorgeous, so benign
I have the luxury to play around with words.

Her father, a judge on the rocky coast of Maine,
was powerless to stop her. His appeals at table

a gruff bluster she could skirt. She just waved
before she gadded off. But then in the blizzard

a mere hundred feet
down slope from Summit House,

its strong tea and heated rocks,
she lay down

and finally tried to answer:
*Here is stone,*

*darkness, wind. My blood*
*flowing slow, my voice*

*already frozen. Father,*
*don't ask*

*for anything more*
*than I can give you now.*

*Sometimes*
*one can only rouse*

*to an even deeper sleep.*
*Father,*

*will your last words*
*be as precious*

*as each one of mine?*

## Spoon River, Personal Mythology, 1988

My old country is Illinois
and in that first year
back from the cabbage and consonant clusters of Poland,
the old wounds of Europe still seeping


and the cold war thawing out in the refrigerator
because of no electricity in our district of Warsaw
I was surrounded by cornfields, by composition students
learning to speak on the page as if it were a foreign tongue.


This is why even now I sing praises to the ladies in their seventies
who signed up for my class at Spoon River College, their talk
of gardens and mason jars, of babies buried in old cemeteries
guarded by the scaly trunks of cedars and poison ivy vines,


the father who bought the first tractor in the county
or the father who drank the whole family down into the ditch.
Each night I read their stories of when they were younger
than I was, of their dark journeys into cellars or the dog


that ran up to them and barked meanly in their face.
It did not bite, but years later they still suffered in their dreams.
And years later I wake up and realize they must be gone,
that I must remember these things for them, even though

I feel too weary to labor past another word, lost in the midst of hogweed, my tongue sharp with the taste of thistle. But when I look down into the well and see only the dankness and the dark, I also hear those women's voices. *Come to the table, come.*

*We will always be able to feed you. But first you must sit down and talk with us again.*

# In the Bottomland

What is in duckweed that sent me down to the slough,
velvet chartreuse on the water, the dark purple underneath
as in the slack rubber of a cottonmouth
before the disturbance? And what caused me
to drive past the gooseneck twist of the river, the pulse
of locusts in the brown-scabbed ghosts of the sycamores, legs
    rubbing
their deafening prayer,
their deafening prayer?

And what caused me to hook one end of a hose
to the exhaust behind my car, snake the other end
through the gapped window? The horseflies
ticked the back glass
then calmed. My head nodded. The deep weeds.
The tiny clay towers
of crawfish. All this I loved
until darkness.

When they removed me
my skin had bubbled like a frog, my eyes bulged.
I left no note. From graveyards
let others sing their songs. But you, little Danny—
though your family drove by on that day
and did not stop to check—have never questioned why
my voice remains
here in the bottomland. Even the doomed can choose
to celebrate their lost worlds, words
ticking like gravel, the Illinois dust
years later, still rising in our throats.

# After Eden

Already in the drowned field they are fishing out
the last of the herd, white necks resting on the trunk
of the stunted mulberry they stood under during rains,
its red and black berries just inches from their lips

as if their appetites reached in that direction.
In life their flood went downward: into grass, the shear
of each green blade that made the cud inside them sharper, the
rumination of those fortunate to survive

until suddenly they are dead.  And we watch it from our house.
Even on dry land, the news is never like promised, the fruit
never close enough that we can eat, the owners
to come along next always wondering whether we too suffered

much before the blow.

# DENSE GROUND

Some years the land sank down in ruts, some years
got dug up and pushed with roots of oak and maple
trees and burned. Some years a seed of corn.
Some years a stalk. Some years the bank called

right when his knees were slick with mud. The grease
was thick but still the metal scraped on metal.
The song got sung, but by whom? The church
of vacant pews, the life of vacant hives?

From wall to wall the dust walked back and forth.
Last night his two-year old was deadly ill
with croup. The man paced the hall, the wheeze
so loud it sounded like it tore apart

the house and farm around him. And then? The blood
was thick, he realized. But dust was even thicker.

# Magnolia Winter

## I

I would like to lead up to this
but I can't. The child

is dead. 1973. Her bicycle already abandoned
amid the silver

forest of parking meters
on the Lawrence County Courthouse

Square, the young part of the year, June,
and this painter guy

who worked on her parents' bedroom
has offered to drive her to Dairy Queen.

*(On the same day the magnolias bloom,*
*the nightcrawlers smear the asphalt,*

*a farm kid downs a six pack*
*and plows his car through the riverside sycamore.)*

So warm for days,
and now the rain splats on every

surface of Illinois.

## II

No, the young girl was not
like a magnolia blossom.

She was a young girl,
murdered and buried.

The painter drove her
on the other side of the Wabash.

Eventually he turned
onto a small road.

## III

It was a cold June
at the Wynoose Tree Nursery.

We jounced off, in the back
of a stock truck, each team

combing the backroads, sheepishly deciding
what they would do

if they had just abducted a young girl:
remembering each dirt and grease road

leading back to an oil tank, rust-sided, in the middle
of old cornstalks not yet plowed under, the road

lubricated to repulse the rain and stave off mud;
each abandoned farm house, its right angles

invaded by tangles of pigweed
and pink wild rose, the uncovered well nearby

a convenient basket for the body; so many choices
leading back

to a field, to a fence-line, to all the various
dead-ends of the earth.

*(And as the season progressed*
*groundhogs newly fattened also*

*developed a knack for dying, their bodies*
*bloating by the side of the road until*

*they could hold nothing more inside.)*
But nothing could prepare us

for the way we gagged, smelling
the burst skin and fur

through the thicket of multi-floral. Luckily,
for us, it was just an animal.

It was some team in Indiana
who noticed the upheaval of dirt behind a log.

IV

Every year the storms come.  The trees
in shreds. A soup of magnolia

blossoms underfoot. The purple finches' nest
under the eaves of the porch

washed out into the thin line of grit
from our curled but intact shingles.

The time of the year when
you don't yet know enough

to name what is your salvation
and what is just a weed.

*(Which stranger will you trust
in your own time of desire? Which friend*

*will end your life as you have known it?)*
Everything is busy

beginning, cleansed with mud, awkward feet
tangled. No wonder only

what gets chosen to live
escapes. The seeds

strewn in shallow graves,
tended. The garden

of that little girl's back
broken

then upturned with a shovel.

## ACHILLES IN THE FENCE ROW

Not the catalpa trees, but the worms themselves, not the worms
but the neighbor girl who slipped them through her lips,
feeling their dry skin, who also kept
toads in plastic easter eggs and checked on them daily,
their growing stink something she could understand
as the days grew longer and her mother disappeared
in a car and did not come back.

Not the fencerows, but the fencerows bulldozed into islands
in the middle of the field. The haven of groundhogs, the tidal
lagoons of their litters, flowing outward
in the sprouts of young corn, their greenness nibbled
into the brownness of dirt. Suddenly our dog would launch out
and I would grab my baseball bat. My dad did not keep guns, so
my job was to get between the whistle pig and its burrow
in the broken trees, to use the swing I learned for little league
to keep our farm from drowning.

Not the sinner but the sin, they said in church. Always the hate
was hated. Not the fact my father died of cancer,
but the fact we lost our farm. Not the fact we finally burned
those hills we made from the trunks of oak or locust,
but the fact that in such burning
you can't avoid to stomp the flames. Two embers crept deep
into my boots, their fangs planted into my ankle. Two scars
I carry to this day.

Not the story you've heard forever, but the story I tell you now.
The story where I mourn my father
never would have the chance to mourn for me. Better
I was a drunken teenager dying on the road.

Better I had leukemia with teddy bears
scattered on my grave. Not the story where I top him, and I
write poems about his death. He should be the one left standing,
his hard trunk declaring protection of our land.

# Ant Farm, Ohio

Barn and church, bridge, windmill with its vane,
stunted maples, the silhouette stark

as a family farm, in a black and white movie, just before
the tornado, one sister reaching the cellar
and one sister not—

    But here,
only a small drizzle sets in as we open the bubble wrap

around a slender vial of ants, settlers
we must stow overnight in our icebox
to slow them down, to be docile

as with the metal tweezers we clutch each thorax
and poke the scrambling pioneer down

into its black entrance. Soon,

they are digging, our son
sings the marching song. The tunnels

go out in all directions, roads
finding the easy way.

*But how can I not write*
*about death?*

Each day the community brings to the surface
a crumpled little gift. A tangle of legs builds up

to become the city dump. Too much food
or too little, the sand now looking like the cracks and smears

on a deer hide
after a hard winter

when the knees finally collapse.

In my hometown in Illinois, a farmer's two root cellars—
catacombs dug

into a creek's ravine—became the crypt

for his two children
dead of diphtheria, black fire and ash

clogging up their lungs. He laid them in there, each
in their own little tube

till the spring thaw, till the ground he farmed more
than he ever talked to his wife

would open to receive them, little boy and girl
who also played with ants, their skinny waists, kneeling in the
    grass,

how they pictured the dark nest
blooming beneath their home. I died with them

every time I heard their story.
                                        And now

back here in Ant Farm, Ohio,
our own son can't wait to tell us

of the latest one he finds, a black puckered thing
blocking the tunnel

toward the main square of the town. *Which way
will they take him,* he says.

*Will the ones who touch him
also start to die?*

# ACKNOWLEDGEMENTS

*2River:* "Ambush Predator"

*Another Chicago Magazine:* "Arch Deluxe"

*Apalachee Review:* "Abandoning the Nest" and "The Winter Too Soon"

*Apple Valley Review:* "The Safety of the Trees"

*Beloit Poetry Journal:* "Absinthe" and "Spit Baths"

*Big Muddy: A Journal of the Mississippi River Valley:* "Spoon River, Personal Mythology, 1988"

*Boxcar Review:* "Ant Farm, Ohio"

*Canary:* "Instinct"

*Central Ohio Writing:* "The Rinsing"

*Chariton Review:* "Contact"

*Cider Press Review:* "Achilles in the Fencerow" and "After Eden"

*Cimarron Review:* "After Supper," "Beatitude," "Fallen Timbers," "One's Tongue," "Student Bride, Indiana University, ca. 1929," and "A Tropic Benediction"

*Conduit:* "The Obligations"

*Confrontation:* "Royal Gorge, Arkansas River, 1959," "On Having a Manger in Our Family Barn (Near Wynoose, Illinois)," and "A Small Prayer"

*Connecticut Review:* "Before the Next Damn Thing Comes," "The Evacuee, Chiricahua Mountains, 2011," and "Flood Stage"

*Connecticut River Review:* "Autobiography with Line-Breaks"

*Farming Magazine:* "The World Writ Large, Writ Small"

*Green Mountains Review:* "The State Trooper Submits His Report"

*Grey Sparrow Journal*: "Lizzie Bourne, Above the Treeline"

*Guernica*: "The Last Bestiary"

*Innisfree Poetry Journal*: "Dead Weight" and "North of Niagara, Bruce Peninsula, I Think of Dead Actors"

*Jelly Bucket*: "Legacy"

*The Journal*: "To the Old Country, Illinois"

*Juxtaprose*: "Against Travel," "The Alien," "Cuneiforms," and "Snow Moon"

*Knockout Literary Review*: "Between Fields"

*Kudzu House Quarterly*: "Car Trouble, Henry Mountains" and "A Man Stacking Stones"

*Lake Effect*: "The Gleaner's Song," "In the Place of Reading the Classics" and "Tea Ceremony"

*Maize*: "The Interior"

*Many Mountains Moving: A Literary Journal of Diverse Contemporary Voices:* "The Life-List"

*Marlboro Review*: "Dense Ground" and "Outings"

*Mid-American Review*: "Definition" and "In the Bottomland"

*Mid-West Quarterly*: "Last Gestures"

*Mississippi Valley Review*: "Plato's Groundhog"

*Pleiades*: "Close Neighbors"

*Plume*: "The Gifts" and "Magnolia Winter"

*Poet Lore*: "The Good Daughter"

*Prairie Schooner*: "Borges, Looking at His Shelves of Books"

*Quarterly West*: "Talking Back to the Exterminator"

*Rhino*: "Stigmata, at Seventeen"

*River Oak Review*: "Near the House," "Still Life with Susan, the Killbuck Marsh, Shreve, Ohio," and "Wild Onion, Easter Sunday"

*Roanoke Review*: "Jewel of Bohemia"

*Salmagundi*: "Patron of the Arts"

*Salt Hill Journal*: "Cave Painting on the Inside of My Skull"

*Soundings Review*: "We Were Going to the Devil"

*Sou'wester*: "All Souls Day, Illinois"

*Tar River Poetry*: "Girl with Bird," "A Long Way Across the Fields," "Mangoes," "Margaret Madly Weeding," "On the Border of New York and Vermont," "Red Sky at Night," and "To the Extinct Aurochs of Europe"

*Tipton Poetry Review*: "In the Last Days, Cardinals" and "The War Home"

*Valparaiso Poetry Review*: "At a Rest Stop Near Lake Erie"

*Weber–The Contemporary West*: "Counting the Coral Beans" and "The Dwellings"

*West Branch*: "Yes, to the Mole, Emerging in Night"

*Zone 3*: "In Charcoal, in March"


"The Safety of the Trees" also won the 2021 *Apple Valley Review's* Editor's Prize and was nominated for a Pushcart Prize

"Secrest Arboretum" appeared in the anthologies *I Have My Own Song For It: Modern Poems of Ohio* (University of Akron Press, Will Greenway and Elton Glaser, eds.) and in *85 Acres on Route 83* (Wooster Book Company, David Wiesenberg, ed.)

"The First of October, We" appeared in the anthology *September 11, 2001: American Writers Respond* (Etruscan Press, William Heyen, ed.)

"A Long Way Across the Fields" was reprinted in *Tar River Poetry's* 30th anniversary commemorative issue

"Wild Onion, Easter Sunday" and "Instinct" were reprinted in the anthology, *Songs for Wild Ohio* (Last Exit Books, R.C. Wilson, ed.)

"Yes, to the Mole, Emerging in Light" was reprinted by *Verse Daily* as its featured poem, June 19, 2004

"The Last Bestiary" was reprinted by *Verse Daily* as its Web Weekly Feature, January 23, 2012

"Ant Farm, Ohio," ("Farma Mrówek w Ohio") also appeared in Poland in the literary magazine *Topos*, translation by Tadeusz Dziewanowski

I would also like to thank the following agencies for their financial and institutional support: the Ohio Arts Council Individual Excellence Awards program; The College of Wooster Henry Luce III Fund for Distinguished Scholarship and The College of Wooster Faculty Development Fund; Joel Bosler-Kilmer in The College of Wooster IT department; and the Lilly Library, Indiana University (where I worked when I discovered the dust jackets from Sylvia Plath's personal library, underneath which she had underlined the books she someday wished to read).

Special thanks too to Margaret Meeker-Bourne, David Wiesenberg, and John Kooistra, among so many others, for their words of wisdom and other guidance in the formation of these poems. And finally, my gratitude to Abigail Warren for her selection of my manuscript as the winner of the 2022 Terry J. Cox Award for poetry, and to Jaynie Royal and Regal House Publishing for their marvelous work in bringing these words into print.